Somewhere Apart

"My Favorite Place in Arkansas"
Arkansas Residents Past and Present

Compiled by
the staff of the *Arkansas Times*
and the staff of
The University of Arkansas Press

The University of Arkansas Press
Fayetteville ✳ 1997

Designed by Liz Lester

⊗ The paper used in this publication meets the minimum requirements of the American National Standard for Permanence of Paper for Printed Library Materials Z39.48-1984.

Library of Congress Cataloging-in-Publication Data

Somewhere apart : "My favorite place in Arkansas" : Arkansas residents past and
    present / compiled by the staff of the Arkansas times and the staff of the
    University of Arkansas Press.
            p.   cm.
        ISBN 1-55728-446-6 (p : alk. paper)
        1. Arkansas—History, Local—Anecdotes. 2. Historic sites—arkansas—
    Anecdotes. 3. Arkansas—Biography—Anecdotes.
    I. University of Arkansas Press. II. Arkansas times (Little Rock, Ark. : 1992)
    F411.6.S66   1997
    976.7—dc21   96–45409
                                                                    CIP

*Map credit (cover): courtesy of the Special Collections Division,
University of Arkansas Libraries, Fayetteville.*

Eureka Springs

Bull Shoals Dam

Cotter

Fayetteville

Drakes Creek

Flat Rock

Boxley

Ozark Folk Center

Blytheville

Cass

Jacksonport

Bayou Bluff

Beebe

Pinnacle Mountain

Marianna

Little Rock

Queen Wilhelmina

Bear Creek Lake

Frazier Lake

Arkansas Post

Dumas

Hope

Camden

Portland

CONTENTS

Preface

Somewhere Apart was originally conceived by the staff of the *Arkansas Times*. Kelley Bass, *Times* feature editor, collected twenty-one essays that appeared in the September 15, 1995, edition under the title "Favorite Places." The authors were given a fairly free hand, asked only to write 50–500 words describing some spot in the state with a special meaning: an unforgettable view, a childhood playground, a hamburger stand—the place one remembers when friends ask about Arkansas, what it is, and why it's special.

The University of Arkansas Press adopted the project and expanded it to become a book covering all corners of the state, from the Ozark Mountains to Dumas, and including a map of Arkansas with the places pinpointed.

But we could not make the book complete; we need the reader's help with that. At the end are blank pages for those special places in each reader's heart.

Jessica White

INTRODUCTION

Neil Compton

    With the passing of the years I have become a rarity in my home state—a life-long Arkansawyer, born in Falling Springs Flats in 1912 and a resident of Arkansas ever since. Today the entire state, and especially our northwest corner, is aswarm with newcomers from states where Arkansas has not always been well understood, misapprehensions arising partly from the fact that Arkansas had been conquered as a southern state, with all the attendant myth, and also that its mostly difficult terrain had left it an arrested frontier in the great land rush to California and sometimes Texas.

This view of backwoods Arkansas has undergone great change in recent years with the appearance of nationally important pace setters in retailing, food production, real estate development, freight hauling, banking and finance, and most surprisingly in politics.

But business and finance and the presidency aside, Arkansas offers something of real value to those who yearn for a chance to enjoy the unspoiled out-of-doors. Our natural state boasts a variety of land forms, many of them denied other states and displayed here in as lovely an arrangement as nature can devise.

Even we natives have been sometimes oblivious to the beauty of the Arkansas landscape. I was in early manhood before I became fully aware of the scenic treasures at our doorstep. To this collection of especially important places may I add my own favorite.

Boxley Valley is a place that has been since the 1830s a home for our first white settlers and before that for the mystical red men who left their little corncobs in Cob Cave as a reminder of their presence here.

My first visit there came at the end of the second World War. I was a discharged naval medical officer on my way home from Little Rock to Bentonville and was intensely interested in what points of natural beauty might lie hidden in our Boston Mountains. With that in mind I took old state highways 21 and 43 from Clarksville to Harrison across that rough country.

It was a trip through yesterday: rail fences, log cabins, one-room schoolhouses and churches, plowmen working fields and gardens, and little country stores at Ozone and Fallsville. Beyond the Mossville church the road plunged downward endlessly from the oak and pinewoods into a forest of great trees, some of them unknown to me. Near the bottom there were fragrant wild azaleas in bloom, a reason to stay for a moment of admiration. There, working on the rutted road, was Jim Lewallen, who wanted to relieve my curiosity, "They was honeysuckles," according to him.

Growing nearby in a damp cleft was a small spreading tree with leaves two feet long and saucer-sized white flowers. That was a "cowcumber tree" Jim had me know, one of our wild magnolias, I would later learn.

At the bottom I had come to the narrow and sheltered valley of the upper Buffalo River. The road crossed the stream on a rusty iron bridge and turned to the north passing a few fields behind sandstone fences and bordered by ancient beech and sweet gum trees in places. Elsewhere there were thickets of redbud and wild plum in bloom. To the west loomed the red ramparts of Moore Creek Bluff and the wooded crest of

Winding Stair Mountain, shutting out the world beyond so recently disrupted by the great war.

In the midst of that peaceful scene, in plain, white-painted elegance, the Boxley community building and church stood guard by the cemetery.

On below were a few well-tended farmsteads with their assorted dwellings and outbuildings, some houses in latter-day bungalow style and others in the older Victorian vernacular. It all blended well with the landscape.

For me it was a fulfillment of those dreams of homecoming during the long months on Guadalcanal. I had come to as lovely a vale as could be found on earth. It was Shangri-la, the Shalimar, the Vale of Tralee. It was a place to restore the troubled spirit of any man. For such a place great soaring passages of music had been written. For such a scene in the Alpine hinterland Beethoven had set down the score for the *Pastoral* Symphony. For such music Boxley Valley was no less an inspiration, and the strains of that music were in my ears on down the road to Ponca.

For me it was a time and place for sincere thanksgiving. For so many of my friends and classmates there would be no homecoming.

For the Lincoln boys, Tommy and Jack (distantly related to Abraham), lost in the air force flying the Hump, and on the ranges of New Guinea.

For Iggy Knott, snuffed out in his parachute harness in Normandy on D-Day.

For my wife's uncle, Carl Swift, downed in a B-24 off Rabaul.

For Dickie Knott, a young genius from Bentonville, shot down by mistake by his own men one dark night in Italy while returning from a reconnaissance assignment.

For A. J. Yates, a Bentonville Tiger and later an All-Star Razorback, killed in a Jeep wreck in North Africa.

And for Dr. H. C. Baker Jr., a class behind me in medical school (and a brother-in-law of Congressman Clyde Ellis), now on the bottom of the Pacific Ocean after the great typhoon.

Today a half century later this valley has changed little but in some respects significantly. As one drops down from the crest of Winding Stair Mountain on smooth new pavement, the great high hills of Cave Mountain and Shiloh shoulder out the horizon and the tiny white community building is seen on the valley floor far below.

There, when about halfway down on the right side of the road, we see a small sign that marks the boundary of the Buffalo National River. Then, on the left, a larger but unobtrusive sign that says Boxley Valley National Historic District placed there by the National Park Service.

Our Buffalo River (the nation's first national river) is in effect a national park extending its 95,000 acres all the way from here down to the White River, but there are within it "historic districts" at Boxley and at Woolum. In these districts, old-time families or even newcomers can own land in fee but such ownership is subject to scenic easement. The landowner is paid a determined amount for which he must agree to not subject the property to commercialism or real-estate development.

Thus Boxley Valley remains much as it was when I first saw it.

Then there is another significant difference. As we proceed on down the road to Ponca, we pass a field on the right. It has been fenced for pasture but at the closed gate we note a group of gawkers looking at something out there. They are elk watchers viewing part of the herd which has been established on the national river and which now numbers 450 head between Boxley and Mt. Hersey.

Each time I travel that road I am grateful that kind fate has permitted me to be a witness to it all.

Now some of my fellow Arkansawyers have *their* favorite places to talk about. Wander on.

Arkansas Post. *Courtesy of the Arkansas History Commission.*

ARKANSAS POST
The Oldest Town of All

Morris S. Arnold

Three hundred and ten years ago, when Europeans first came here to stay, Arkansas Post was out in the middle of nowhere and it still is. One goes there deliberately, on purpose: it is not easy to stumble on accidentally, and it is not on the way to anywhere else. Settled long before St. Louis, and a healthy three or four decades older even than New Orleans, the old town was the scene of at least three bona fide battles, including one during the American Revolution when French militiamen, Spanish troops, and Quapaw Indians fought back a British and Chickasaw force with cannon, swivel guns, muskets, pistols, tomahawks, and anything else they could lay their hands on.

It is on this seventeenth- and eighteenth-century foundation that the mind's eye may prefer to focus when visiting the Post. There was a Civil War redoubt here, to be sure, but that era is too recent (mere journalism, really), and too redolent with current political concerns, for comfortable rumination. (The real Confederate flag does not fly here, only some unfamiliar and antiseptic bunting, bereft of ideology, that, they say, the Confederate Congress once approved as a symbol for their stillborn nation.) The French Louisiana village is gone, for all intents and purposes a casualty of this Civil War, when Union gunboats reduced the creaky colonial houses to dust. Even so, a resolute United States Post Office continued to maintain that there was a town here until 1934, and as recently as 1980 the geological survey maps faithfully recorded a ghost of a settlement (three or four houses) bearing the ancient name.

Now, as with much else, the federal government has taken possession, and helpful park rangers preside over a fine, well-kept brick building with exhibits on the fur and skin trade and a little theater that features a slide show. Behind the building, sidewalks channel visitors through the town site, and a few signs along the way help guide the imagination but do not intrude upon it. The sheer range of what occurred here during the course of four different centuries makes for a vigorous struggle in the mind.

There is the founder of the Post, Henri de Tonty, who lost his right hand to a grenade in Sicily, and whom the Indians called "Iron Hand" because of the prosthetic that he wore. There is Jean-Baptiste Bénard de La Harpe, whose name now graces a major street in Little Rock and whose ambitious exploration of the Arkansas River came a cropper not far from the city. There is Jean-François Dumont de Montigny, who wrote some execrable French verses about Arkansas while he was here but who is withal amusing and engaging. There is Jean-Bernard Bossu, forever the self-absorbed huckster for whom fact and fantasy were evidently indistinguishable, who gave us engravings of the Quapaws and two books full of truthful detail and much disinformation. There is the pirate Jean Lafitte, fomenting disaffection among the abandoned French. There is the naturalist Thomas Nuttall, a quintessential Harvard Pecksniff who nevertheless left us affecting descriptions of a prelapsarian land now irredeemably lost. There is even Washington Irving, who used the Post to contrast the *habitants* of the sleepy Creole villages of colonial Louisiana with the boisterous, westering republicans who were soon to engulf them for good.

Some other names come to mind, virtually unpronounceable names that are just now being rescued from obscurity, names like Guedelonguay, Zenomony, Pasimony, Huatirouinonzis, and Huahitaze, Quapaw chiefs all, who lived symbiotically with their French and Spanish neighbors for upwards of six generations, giving the lie to much recent polemical writing that posits unrelenting conflict between Indians and Europeans on a genocidal scale. These Quapaws sometimes seem irretrievably lost to us, buried at first under layers of unsympathetic commentary by uncomprehending Europeans, and now exploited by social critics who invest them with all the qualities that we modern Americans supposedly lack (an ecologically correct Pocahontas?)—exactly as the *philosophes,* including our own Bossu, had done two hundred years and more before.

All these and dozens of others have provided us with a lifetime of wondering, their scattered reminiscences so personal and eccentric that even the most watchful skepticism cannot always tease the truth from them. And beyond them, a background barely visible in the half-light, of tall, brown prairie sage, black with red-tongued buffalo, slumbering bears, bucks with hooves like hail and breath like smoke, pale does moving quietly, swiftly, barely touching the horizon.

A retreat from places long on science and short on appetite.

Morris S. Arnold, a native of
Texarkana, sits on the United
States Court of Appeals for the
Eighth Circuit. He is the author
of a number of books and articles
on legal history and colonial
Arkansas. His most recent book
is *Colonial Arkansas, 1686–1804:
A Social and Cultural History.*

THE OLD STATE HOUSE

Noble and Majestic

Dee Brown

Down in south Arkansas an old country church was once my favorite place in the state, but the building has long since vanished, and the church-yard has been absorbed back into the pine forest from which it was taken almost a century ago. My favorite place in the Ozarks was a village set definitely in place and time, a nineteenth-century collection of buildings and people—changeless I foolishly believed. It, too, has vanished, replaced by transitory modernity.

Because it is not easy to retain in the mind's eye a favorite place that no longer exists, I have fixed upon an urban locale and a building that has existed far longer than I and promises to remain long after I'm gone. This is a noble structure designed by an architect named Gideon Shryock. (Printers usually misspell his last name.) It stands on Markham Street between the end of Center Street and the riverfront. Presently it is called the Old State House, but when I first knew it the name was War Memorial Building. Before then it was the state capitol, built long before the Civil War.

Although the building needed paint and repairs when I first fell in love with it, something about its form and lines and the majestic columns struck my youthful fancy. My first entry was from the riverside, the rear entrance to what was then the state medical school. On a dare I went with two older schoolboys to secretly view cadavers floating in a tank of dark evil-smelling liquid. Some years later, I was using the front entrance to investigate Civil War records which were housed in the building after the medical school was relocated.

Today the Old State House is a grand museum of history, all dressed up like a duenna with new body parts and a face lift. Yes, there is something feminine about Mr. Shryock's building, but the floors still creak with life and history, and she is my favorite place in the state of Arkansas.

Courtesy of August House Publishers, Inc.

Dee Brown is probably best known for *Bury My Heart at Wounded Knee: An Indian History of the American West.* He is the author of more than a dozen other books on the Old West, for adults and children.

Helen Gurley Brown,
author of seven books
on the ways of women
in the contemporary
world, was born in
Green Forest, Arkansas.
She was an advertising
copywriter in Hollywood
before becoming editor
of *Cosmopolitan* in 1965.

Arkansas

There's No Place Like Home

Helen Gurley Brown

I'm sure this is very clichéd, but nothing is more beautiful than Eureka Springs and the Ozark Mountains in the fall. It's so satisfying, very different from what one usually sees in the world. We have fall and changing leaves in New York, but nothing as spectacular as that. I know Hot Springs is still very charming, and I have happy memories of going to the races at Oaklawn every Saturday afternoon as a girl. Last year I visited Little Rock for the first time in thirty years and found it hospitable, friendly, and very southern. I love just running around the city—western Little Rock, especially, which has become so posh and beautiful.

Bayou Bluff

The Beauty and Darkness of Nature

John Churchill

Arkansas has a rough sort of beauty that often bears a sting or an itch. A field lush with wildflowers will turn out to be full of chiggers and seed ticks. An evening on the porch listening to the crickets and the whippoorwills will be punctuated by the regular slapping of mosquitos—a process that, when successful, gives us the odd glimpse of a speck of our own blood, fresh from the guts of another creature. Beyond the presence of the unsettling, the beauties of Arkansas can even be fatal. Newspapers are full of stories about people drowning in lakes and streams, pitching off magnificent bluffs, and struck dead by lightning in the middle of a spectacular thunderstorm. By providing plenty of annoying insects, as well as mortal danger,

Arkansas saves us from being lulled into a sappy romanticism about Nature. It offers instead the opportunity for a rich appreciation of Nature's ambivalences, her webbing of beauty with darker elements.

Arkansas readily offers parallel cultural ambivalences. Little in our history conjures a nostalgia untinged by some version of regret. Our distinctive accents and manners are hard to define. They fade into those of neighbors on every border, just as the land merges with Missouri and Oklahoma and the waters pour to Mississippi and Louisiana. Too often we imagine these mixed feelings as obstacles to an understanding of the state. I don't think so. Because of these ambivalences and not despite them, I count myself lucky to be rooted here and to find my heart fixed to a place that embodies them. My favorite place in Arkansas is Bayou Bluff, a spot at the southern edge of the Ozarks.

About sixteen miles west of Conway, Interstate 40 crests a ridge and the view opens to the north toward White Oak Mountain on the furthest horizon. This country is drained by streams that rise steep, clear, and rock-strewn, making their way by bluffs into the lower hills, turning gradually sluggish and moccasin-colored as they join the Arkansas River. The ambiguities of this transition are captured in the place name of Bayou Bluff.

At the foot of White Oak Mountain, the last town with a school, stores, and a post office is Hector. From there, Highway 27 twists through the valley of the Illinois Bayou for a few miles before climbing to the plateau above. Just at the point where the road leaves the creek to go up the hill, there is an old cedar-shaded cemetery and beside it a campground on a low, ragged bluff. Below the bluff is the bayou, fresh from its descent from the mountain, headed south into canebrakes and cypresses.

I used to be intent on encounters with pristine Nature. That was before I understood that this notion is a dangerous fantasy, a part of the myth that pretends that humans are not at home in the world. But the fact that we are at home here means that the world is freighted with human meaning. Things have happened here. Mossy banks are places where we could lie down, where we have lain, where others, after, will lie. Here, in a pool of clear, cool, summer water, I learned to swim. When my grandfather died and all the cousins ran the well dry, we went to bathe there in the moonlight. I flee to Bayou Bluff from the world of books and committees, and it is the sort of place my grown son refers to when he says, "It feels like where I'm from." Jean and I have taken our children there again and again in the hope that they would learn what it feels like to be in this place. But it is not a place of benign beauty. Half of what grows is poison ivy, and you must watch where you put your feet. You learn never to put your hand on a ledge you cannot see.

The colors there are oak-leaf green and water green, cedar green and moss, the slaty gray of the rock and the gray-white of lichen, the motley red-brown and weathered gray of cedar bark, and the red of the dirt that runs in seams through the bluff, washing out into a gritty sand and leaving the rocks to fall into the creek in the next storm.

On every visit I find that some new rock, large or small, has fallen off the bluff, and left a hole above where there will be more washing out as the ancient process of taking these hills slowly down and down goes on. In the flood of 1982 the whole creek was rearranged, and my childhood swimming hole was filled with rocks. Someone else might regret these changes. Not me. I like the way the bayou shows the earth itself at work, or being worked on—piling up here, pulling down there. Paying attention to this process can correct our tendency to value only what promises to last forever. Even the mountains are coming down. You can see it at Bayou Bluff, though you have to watch for a long time.

Being in a place like this can help you get a sense for things that take a long time—a lifetime, or more. I come here and think of the people who came: the Cherokee who were moved through and my ancestors who followed and stayed only until paved roads made it easy to leave. I think about the academic life I have and the projects I work on, many of which take a long time and embody a dangerous and annoying beauty. I think about my grandfathers who were storekeepers in Hector; my grandmothers who raised families and tended gardens, roses, and chickens; their parents who were farmers; and theirs who came from Mississippi, Tennessee, and the Carolinas. I think about the storms whose waters wear down the land. Cliché or not, it is true: I think of myself as a child lying on a pallet at my grandparents' house, listening to summer storms batter on the tin roof, and then also of the same storms crashing these last nights around my house in Conway. All this gathers for me at Bayou Bluff, and for that reason it is my favorite place.

John Churchill was born in
Hector, Arkansas, and grew up
there and in Little Rock. He
lives in Conway with his wife,
Jean, and their children, Will,
Mary Katherine, and Hugh.
A member of the faculty of
Hendrix College since 1977,
John is the academic vice
president and dean of the
college and a professor of
philosophy. He usually
writes on liberal arts and
topics in the philosophy
of religion.

EUREKA SPRINGS
Home, Apparently

Crescent Dragonwagon

    I kept a minimal diary then. I was nineteen, washed up onto the shores of Eureka Springs, unsure, wanting to write, recovering from having been the victim of a violent crime months earlier. My recognition of Eureka was immediate. "Eureka Is Great," I wrote that day, January 7, 1972. "Home, apparently. I'm not going to go west. Found a place. New beginnings. About time."

    From my first walk in the town that would become my home, how moving and timeless the narrow street seemed, curving uphill, with its Victorian stone buildings. The old city was deserted, its out-of-time, peculiar atmosphere as palpable as the needle-fine rain misting my face that day under the gray sky.

Photograph by Susan Storch.

Remember, it was January 1972. Deep off-season. What few shops existed, in that preboom, prerenovation-conscious Eureka, were closed. There were almost no people on the street, which was why I was puzzled by some faint, convivial sounds coming from somewhere unseen. Just as I reached the bend that curves Spring Street into a sinuous, traffic-slowing angle, I saw a single illuminated shop, from which the sounds were issuing. Butter-yellow light poured from the plate-glass window, the sole luminescence that gray afternoon on the empty archaic street. That, and the sounds, drew me into the tiny coffee shop, long, narrow, filled with conversation, laughter, someone playing the guitar. It was aromatic, steamy from an enormous brass-and-copper espresso machine, and filled with eight or ten people, most young, long-haired, in denim.

Someone asked me my name, where I was from. I told him, or her, and that I'd just arrived. I can't recall who asked me; I doubt he, or she, is still here, since I do recall those from that era who are—several would turn out to be my partners in our mutual growing up. What I do remember is this: the smell of wet wool and woodsmoke, so distinctive a Eureka Springs–people odor, not at all unpleasant; that smell of whoever it was that wrapped their arms around me and hugged me, hard.

Whoever it was said, "Welcome home, Crescent."

I'm forty-two now and still here.

These days, the town's much more touristy. After the spectacular scenery and winding curves of the up-and-down Ozark roads coming in, there's a ring of neon, aluminum siding, fast-food places—strip development, modified with hillbilly, religious, and pseudo-Victorian motifs. Corn-dog emporia and yard-ornament places vie with country-music shows and motels. I'd be lying if I said it doesn't bother me that when I drive to Berryville now (a route that when I first arrived sported only pine trees and a lone Western Auto) I pass through all these "meat by-products of tourism," as Mel White described 'em.

But lately I've been trying to look at it as Americana, high camp, proof of the fact that Eureka Springs will never suffer from an inflated view of its own perfect tastefulness, like Santa Fe. And further, every motel owner and t-shirt shop owner is pursuing his or her dreams here, too, just as I was and am. As I witness myself wrestling with my own snobbish aesthetic concerns, trying to temper them with a little tolerance, humility, and maturity, I am reminded of the transcendentalist Margaret Fuller, who announced ringingly one day, "I accept the universe!" Thomas Carlyle is reputed to have growled in response, "She'd damn well better."

Living here so long, arriving when and as I did, it's a considerable struggle to avoid that most seductive and legitimate of unhappinesses, nostalgia. But the fact is, I *am* happy, more or less, with my goofy, contentious, beautiful, tacky little town. I loved Eureka then and now for some of the same, and some different, reasons. The city, after all, is not one place but at least two, probably many. And however you feel about what is universally referred to as "up on the highway," you can always keep going till you get to the sign that says "Historic District." Turn right; go down the hill. You'll find a cross between *Brigadoon* and Lake Woebegone with plenty of *Northern Exposure* thrown in, set in rugged, green, hilly countryside, dotted with springs and rock bluffs. Scatter this terrain with Victorian houses and commercial buildings clinging up and down the hollows in visual defiance of common sense, city planning, and gravity. Add tiny landscaped parks, elegant gray retaining walls of Eureka-quarried limestone. Add our wildly diverse population; and if you scratch any of us locals a little deeper than "How do you get to the Passion Play?" you will add just these intoxicating eccentricities to your travel experiences.

If the town no longer cures physical diseases (including, according to the accounts, everything from scrofula and malaria to, as the Victorians delicately put it, "gentleman's inability"), it relieves other modern afflictions. Fear of crime, alienation, and disorientation in a too big, too fast world, the anxiety that sets in when everything, from motels to airports to fast-food restaurants, looks like everything else, everywhere: these uneasinesses are what Eureka cures now, still.

Eureka looks, tastes, and smells different because it is. The streets still double back on themselves; the view from the East Mountain overlook stills astonishes; the woods are still crosshatched with walking paths. I always suggest visitors get a massage, eat a really good meal of *slow* food at any of a dozen or so chef-owned restaurants, buy something made and sold only right here, nap, relax.

I think mostly we Eurekans realize we're all healing from something, and that on this brief, mysterious, lush sojourn through our lives, we are all tourists. Eureka's got a long tradition of helpfulness in this regard.

Welcome home.

Crescent Dragonwagon is a novelist and children's author. She and her husband run Dairy Hollow House, a bed-and-breakfast in Eureka Springs.

OZARK FOLK CENTER
Come and Sit a Spell

Jimmy Driftwood

Your favorite place should be where you eat and sleep. If my favorite place in Arkansas wasn't right here in the Ozarks, I would have left a long time ago. I would have gone somewhere else to sing my songs. I wouldn't have done all the work I've done here with the Ozark Folk Center (in Mountain View), and if you come up here to Stone County and see everything that's happened to our part of the country in the past forty years, you'd understand why and how much I love it.

Jimmy Driftwood is a singer and songwriter with roots that run deep in the music of the American South. Among his better known songs is "The Battle of New Orleans." He lives in Timbo.

BEEBE

The Grove

George Fisher

Dad often said that when the Great Depression visited our part of the country, we were not aware of its arrival, since we had always been poor. Poor but not paupers. The Olmsteads owned about twenty acres between our home and theirs that we all called the "Grove." Part of the Grove was cleared off for baseball. Stately trees, under which we played marbles and other kid games, covered the rest of it. Eddie MacBee, a former Chicago White Sox pitcher, played for the Beebe team. He taught me how to throw a curve. We were both lefties.

Plenty happened in the Grove for the townsfolk—picnics, ball games, minicarnivals, and so on. We kids picked up half-smoked cigarettes after

The Grove

the events and smoked them later in our barns. Old Golds and Chesterfields were our favorite brands.

I was popular with everyone because I could draw. "You sure can draw good," my contemporaries would say. Some of the wealthier people in town noticed my drawing ability and suggested they might send me off to get art training, but my dad objected. I never knew why, but maybe the reader will know. Dad was fiercely proud of his kids. My mother died when I was five. Dad labored to get me to understand politics and history, which got me started in a field of art related to editorial comment.

I think the first years of our lives, whether rich or poor, are the happiest—when you can act like grown-ups and build things like grown-ups have. Paul Olmstead and I built airplanes that never flew, started our own hospital but never charged for our services, built our own fire trucks, and set fire to fields so we could put them out. We put nails in our shoes from the inside out to look like we were wearing pro baseball spikes. We even built our own sophisticated rubber guns and had gang wars.

As we sat on the foot-worn roots under the big shady oaks in the Grove, we'd often imagine what each would want to be: a locomotive engineer, an army officer, a truck driver. Paul wanted to be a big-league baseball player. I wanted to be a newspaper cartoonist.

George Fisher was for years political cartoonist for the *Arkansas Gazette.* His award-winning work now appears in the *Arkansas Times* and in syndication. The University of Arkansas Press has published three volumes of his cartoons.

Photograph by Kathy Hinson.

FAYETTEVILLE

My Backyard

Ellen Gilchrist

My favorite place in Arkansas is my backyard. There are generations of squirrels, rabbits, mockingbirds, cardinals, blue jays, itinerant turtles, possums, and an occasional armadillo—not to mention the roadrunner who took up residence on my roof. These animals serve as my pets. They are extremely low-maintenance. They feed themselves, fight among themselves without bothering me, kill bothersome insects, and shun the snake who lives in the stone wall. He is a handsome, lonely creature, guarding his treasure year after year. He guards about two square feet of land covered with rocks and hickory nuts that have been turned silver by a steady stream of Clorox-treated water from inside the house. It is a crazy house, a mad creation of

"Yard with Visitors"

the genius Faye Jones, which I have significantly altered to fit my needs and fancies.

I am involved in the lives of these creatures. This morning I saw an adolescent mockingbird on the very top of a young pine tree. He was born and raised not twelve feet away from my dining-room table. I have watched him take many meals from his mother's beak. Now he is preening himself on the pine and getting his own worms and caterpillars.

These descendents of the dinosaurs fascinate me. I am dazzled by their independence and ingenuity, their beauty and single-mindedness. Hunger is a mighty force, and they are always hungry. I like to watch them build their nests. Some of them are good at it. Others are too inept to be pitied. I watched a robin build a nest so sloppy, out on such an undependable limb, that I wasn't even sorry when the first big wind carried it away.

I am also involved in the lives of my neighbors. One is a painter and a great one. Another grows outrageously beautiful flowers. I pretend to be insanely jealous of his blooms. He tells stories all over town about my sloppy watering techniques.

This is my life, and this is where I lead it. This means a great deal to me since it is the closest I have come to Zen, to the heart of saying *be here now.*

I moved around all my life. My father bought a dozen beautiful houses in a dozen towns. As soon as I would begin to know a place, I would leave. This made me powerful and free in many ways. It also made me rootless like the gardenias I keep trying to grow in the rocky soil beside the mailbox.

I am flourishing in the state of Arkansas on the acre of land I bought with the fruits of my labors and with the trees I planted, my snake, the visiting roadrunner, and the children who use my yard as a shortcut to grammar school. I'm starting to take root. I can leave my driveway and drive down to the Fayetteville square and see three people I know on the way. I can go to the bookstore and see four more. I can go to the coffee shop and find company any time of the day. My grandchildren come here to visit. They think it is Shangri La. We drive up to the Smokehouse on Highway 71, which Clarence Hall calls the Death Highway. We look out over the unspoiled vistas. I love this place so much I don't want to talk about it. When I die, make a pyre of yellow leaves and burn me in my backyard. Don't bother to scatter the ashes. The wind and rain will take care of that. I live in a glass house in a place that has thunderstorms and constant tornado warnings. I never lack for excitement or chances to prove my bravery. Once, at dusk, there were sirens and strange spotlights in the air. At that time I was refusing to have a television set, so I got in the car and drove down to Jim and Gen Whitehead's house to see if a nuclear war had started. "No," they told me. "It's the mall. They're having an opening at the mall." Since then I have ridden out emergencies in my own place. I open the doors to the yard. I get in the bed. I decide to assume I'm safe. If the mockingbirds can brave it, so can I.

Photograph by Don House.

Ellen Gilchrist's novels and short stories have garnered a great number of honors, including the American Book Award in 1984. For some time she was a commentator on National Public Radio's *Morning Edition.*

Photo by S. Walker.

VETERANS' CEMETERY

A Father Rests Peacefully

George W. Haley

On whatever occasions I can, I visit my father's grave at the Veterans' Cemetery in Little Rock where we laid him to rest after his many years of teaching at Arkansas AM&N (Arkansas Agricultural, Mechanical, and Normal College, presently known as the University of Arkansas at Pine Bluff). I go there simply for the inspiration and solace that it provides. It seems almost a religious place, one inviting contemplation. Sometimes, when Dad and I commune, I can almost hear him singing "Danny Boy," his favorite song. Oftentimes in that place, amid so much that has passed before, complex problems become less so, and solutions reveal themselves. I know we all have our favorite places, but this is mine.

George W. Haley attended school
in Pine Bluff and took his law
degree from the University of
Arkansas. He served as
chairman of the Postal Rate
Commission, of which he is
presently a commissioner.

DRAKES CREEK

Stay More

Donald Harington

In all the world the spot I most like to frequent I have never actually visited: the mind of my reader, *you,* if you will, if you have ever inhabited in your reading the village of Stay More, Arkansas.

I wish I could see it through your eyes. I'd like to know the shades of green that your mind colors the lush vegetation, the fragrances that you detect in the first morning air, the sounds you hear in the still of evening, the sense you have of never knowing just how you got there and never wanting, ever, to leave.

But this world that my words have spun around you belongs to you alone, and I can only pretend to visit it, with some of the joyful suspension-of-disbelief that you yourself choose to exercise when you find yourself in

Stay More. It is my pretense of visiting your mind, which I indulge in every day I sit down to write, that keeps the town alive.

On occasion you will ask me, "Was there ever anywhere a *real* place like Stay More?" While the question flatters me with the implication that I've made the town so true for you that you want to know just *where* it is, it saddens me with the burden of the answer: no, I can't draw you a map for finding the real Stay More (because, I am always tempted to parentheticize, all nine of my novels will get you to Stay More faster than any map).

I can, however, tell you that if you look hard enough, you can find *aspects* of Stay More in three separate spots, all within an hour's leisurely drive of each other and of Fayetteville, where I live. First, there is the Ozark village of my boyhood, now a ghost town (almost). At one time, Drakes Creek had a population of five hundred and was the third largest town in Madison County. Its main street was such a thriving commercial district that people spoke of "Draketown" to set it off from the rest of the sprawling town, and that nickname still exists, although the main street itself is closed off from the nearby paved highway which cut a gouge through the hill behind the village.

Only one building is left—a handsome two-story carpenter-Gothic house, lovingly restored in recent years by a herbalist, Mrs. Lewis. It once was Drakes Creek's hotel, and in the years of my growing up it belonged to my grandmother, Mrs. Minnie Nail, who let me have the best upstairs room for my own. From my window I could see the huge general store across the road, the shell of the bank building, the ruin of the four-story gristmill, and the doctor's office. All of these are gone now.

I loved that house so much I used it as Governor Jacob Ingledew's trigeminal house in my novel *The Architecture of the Arkansas Ozarks,* and I drew a picture of it which illustrates chapter 7 of that book. In my picture I forgot to include the porch swing at the right end of the porch, a swing which figures prominently in other of my novels, and a swing in which I had my first taste of some great writers like Dostoyevsky, Twain, Faulkner, and Styron.

That house is also the main setting, called "Holy House," of my fable, *The Cockroaches of Stay More.* I once wanted to live there again, as Larry Brace did, but Mrs. Lewis beat me to it. For that matter, it is the final home of the title character of *Ekaterina,* and the full story of her occupancy of it remains to be told.

The hills surrounding Drakes Creek are gentle and unspectacular, although as a boy I thought of them as "mountains," just as the settlers who named them did. But for Stay More we need higher mountains, deeper hollers, and a greater variety of the profile or skyline of the ridges.

That is one reason that geographically and topographically, in order to create Stay More, I moved Drakes Creek one county eastward (just as Faulkner had moved his "Jefferson" one county eastward into Yoknapatawpha). It is thus "located" approximately in the vicinity of the ghost village of Murray, southeast of Parthenon (an actual village which appears as such in all my books). Murray never was much of a town, as towns go, and you won't find anything there to suggest Stay More . . . except the absolutely gorgeous scenery, the beautiful Little Buffalo River, "Leapin' Rock," and the trees, shrubs, flowers, and all.

Several of the few residents of that part of Newton County are readers, and they have come to think of their countryside as "Stay More." I'm pleased and, at the same time, I'm envious of their actual physical inhabitance of a magical place that you and I must fabricate in our enchanted brains.

To get an idea of what Stay More (or Drakes Creek) actually looked like during its thriving heyday, you can head back into eastern Madison County to the remote but still active town of Kingston. This thoroughly charming village still has a "square" of sorts with buildings on four sides, including a still-serving cafe (where once I ordered peach "clobber" from the menu), a still-paying bank, and even a still-fixing auto mechanic running "Malfunction Junction."

You'll wonder how a village of such substantial commerce could still be surviving in such a remote location, and indeed present-day Kingston is a much-diminished relic of a town which once had *three* drugstores, a movie theater, four cafes, two millineries, a hotel, a hospital, et cetera, et cetera. But it's *there,* and would even make a good movie set if they covered the now-paved streets with dirt.

The streets of Stay More will never be paved. They will always, as they've been doing, make a wonderful movie set for the enduring and endearing movies of your mind in which you are the director, cinematographer, grip, best boy, and everything else . . . except scriptwriter, which I'll always be.

Photo by Kim Harington.

Donald Harington was born in Little Rock in 1935 and currently lives in Fayetteville with his wife, Kim, and teaches art history at the University of Arkansas. Throughout his childhood, he summered in the Ozark hamlet of Drakes Creek. With his 1970 novel, *Lightning Bug,* Harington introduced the invented hamlet of Stay More, the capital seat of his imagination, set in the Ozarks of Arkansas.

THE WHITE RIVER
A River Runs Deep in Me

Wayland Holyfield

Wildcat, Buffalo, Rim, and Roundhouse. Not to be confused with those found in zoos, canyons, and railroad yards. No, these are wonderfully descriptive names of fast-water shoals that always trigger in me special memories of one of my favorite places, the White River in northern Arkansas.

I will never forget, as a teenage boy, wading into Rim Shoals in tennis shoes and jeans and waiting for my legs to get numb so I could endure fishing that stretch of icy-cold water. With a heavy old fiberglass fly rod, rusty reel, and sinking fly line (not on purpose), I would spend hours stalking and trying to cast a big black wooly worm fly for very wary rainbow trout. The fishing was always good. The catching was usually not.

Since those days, I've had the opportunity to lay out lines on some of the most famous trout waters in North America. (I guess the work schedule of a songwriter does have some advantages.) I still consider my Arkansas White River one of the great fisheries and memory makers in the United States of America.

Recently, on one of my return visits to the river, I stood on the bank in my neoprene waders, holding my graphite fly rod, armed with a hardy reel and sixty-dollar fly line, and watched a sixteen-year-old boy wade into Wildcat Shoals. Silhouetted against the fog and mist, he quietly fished and laid cast after cast with a grace and patience that would make a dad proud. And I was.

I don't recall how many (if any) fish were caught, but I do know the fishing was particularly great that day.

A lot of water has run over Bull Shoals Dam since my teenage times on the White and something tells me from my last trip with my son, Mark, that he will carry on my special feeling for a very special place where the fishing and the memories are always good.

Wayland Holyfield is a native of Little Rock and lives in Nashville. He is a member of the Nashville Songwriter's Association Hall of Fame and has written fourteen number one songs including the Grammy winning "Could I Have This Dance?" sung by Anne Murray. He also wrote and sang "Arkansas, You Run Deep in Me," which was adopted as the state song in 1988.

FRAZIER LAKE
Calm and Restful

George Howard Jr.

The White River National Wildlife Refuge is my and my wife's favorite fishing area during the summer months—specifically, Frazier Lake, which is located just east of DeWitt, Arkansas, a part of approximately ten thousand acres of lakes and streams in the refuge, is our choice and most liked. While moving quietly and peaceably in our boat around the huge and beautiful cypress trees, which offer a calm and restful surrounding, we are removed for a brief period from the problems and frustrations of everyday living and reap joyfully some of the extraordinary benefits that nature has in store for humankind, including some of those mouthwatering bream, crappie, and bass. In my humble judgment, the accompanying photograph depicts this calm and restful atmosphere.

George Howard Jr. is a native of
Pine Bluff, where he practiced
law before his appointment to
the Arkansas Supreme Court
and then as a federal judge for
the eastern district, seated
in Little Rock.

LITTLE ROCK

Where the Wildflowers Grow

Carl Hunter

     Since I am interested in the wildflowers of Arkansas, I naturally think of places where I have seen an abundance of these when I try to decide upon my favorite place in the state.

     One of the places is the wildflower glen at Wildwood on Denny Road, west of Little Rock. I have listed over ninety wildflower species there. Some are unusual, such as Indian pink, yellow indigo, and Indian plantain. Others are more common and are familiar to most people, including black-eyed Susan, coreopsis, bachelor's button, and Queen Anne's lace.

     There is a level trail that is only two hundred yards long from which all of these wildflowers can be seen. The best season is from early spring until July.

Wendy Welch planted wildflowers around the edges of this area, and she had the good judgment to plant species native to Arkansas. I will be planting fall wildflowers to extend the blooming season at this garden spot. The potential for wildflowers here and the opportunity for everyone to enjoy them are two more reasons why this is one of my favorite places in Arkansas.

Carl Hunter is a naturalist who has authored books on the wildflowers, shrubs, and trees of Arkansas.

Sketch by J. D. Ashley.

JACKSONPORT

Everybody Needs a Laughing Place!

Elizabeth Jacoway

At the confluence of the White and Black Rivers, in the backwater of the Mississippi Delta where white and black cultures mingle in the traditional southern pattern, the crown jewel of the Arkansas state park system glistens and beckons along the lush riverbanks at Jacksonport. The old courthouse museum, the imposing Confederate monument, the stern-wheeler steamboat, the wildflower walk, the RV campgrounds, the picnic pavilion, and the long sandy beach offer the visitor or the native a variety of pleasures for mind, body, and soul.

Once a thriving commercial center and a transshipment point for White River plantation cotton, the struggling Jacksonport community is now a monument to the poor business sense of the Arkansas planter. When the Cairo and Fulton Railroad plotted its course through eastern Arkansas in the early 1870s, it asked the town fathers for twenty-five thousand dollars to secure a rail route through Jacksonport. Prospering from the well-established steamboat traffic and lacking a vision of their economy's future, the town fathers declined. The railroad went through Newport, and Jacksonport died.

Lady Elizabeth Watson Luker, the great-granddaughter of one of Jacksonport's founders, who also happened to be the granddaughter of the Confederate general who led the Jackson Guards off to war from that very shore, created at Jacksonport a testament to the impact that one person of imagination and force can have when she "blooms" where she is planted. Recognizing the old courthouse as a treasure in ruins, she persuaded skeptical Jackson County neighbors that the decaying building at Jacksonport that had been used for decades as an old folks' home and even a grain storage facility *could* be made into a museum and that with their funds and backing it *should* be restored.

Never flagging in her enthusiasm, the aptly named Lady Elizabeth created the Jackson County Historical Society, wrote a history of the Civil War in Jackson County entitled *Fight and Survive!,* and used the proceeds to support her burgeoning museum project. She then acquired and restored a steamboat—the *Mary Woods 2*—which she turned into a one-of-a-kind steamboat museum, and persuaded her friend Jimmy Wilmans to donate a gorgeous expanse of land for an extensive riverfront park. In time the state rewarded her efforts by designating the Jacksonport creation a state park in 1965. Since then the park and museum at Jacksonport has been recognized repeatedly as one of the premier tourist attractions in Arkansas.

Today, Jacksonport is very busy year-round, though the steamboat museum is open only in the summer. Visitors to the courthouse can learn about life in eastern Arkansas from period rooms; a restored courtroom and doctor's office; an extensive collection of military uniforms, weapons, and supplies; an equally impressive collection of ladies' and childrens' clothing; an exhibit of agricultural implements; and much more. Whether it's a community Christmas party in the courtroom, a wedding on the grounds of this imposing and beautifully restored edifice, a family reunion in the pavilion, a sunrise Eucharist above the river, a quiet walk along the Boy Scout trail, or a full-fledged peoples' festival—Portfest—along the riverbank, the state park at Jacksonport is a happy place to be. Everybody needs a laughing place, and this is the one for me!

Elizabeth Jacoway is a former associate professor of history at the University of Arkansas at Little Rock. She has served as president of the Arkansas Women's History Institute in 1985 and 1986 and of the Southern Association for Women Historians in 1981. A specialist in the fields of southern history and race relations, she is the author of *Yankee Missionaries in the South: The Penn School Experiment* (Louisiana State University Press, 1981), the editor (with David Coburn) of *Southern Businessmen and Desegregation* (Louisiana State University Press, 1981), the editor of *"Behold, Our Works Were Good!": A Handbook of Arkansas Women's History* (August House, 1986), and the editor (with Dan Carter, Lester Lamon, and Robert McMath) of *The Adaptable South: Essays in Honor of George Brown Tindall* (Louisiana State University Press, 1991). Although she has aspirations of getting back to writing, these days she is mostly a mom to her two boys, Tim Jr. and Todd Watson. She lives in Newport.

LITTLE ROCK

Barbershop Blues

Henry L. Jones Jr.

As a child, I was accompanied by my father to the barbershop where, although haircuts were given, much, much more than the simple cutting of hair drew my attention and filled me with excitement and wonder. The men who always happened to be present when my father took me there were men I saw on other occasions at church, in stores or homes, and at many other places doing ordinary things.

When I saw these men in the barbershop, however, they were magically transformed into the most knowledgeable persons one could ever imagine. They knew all about politics, medicine, law, government, religion, and every

65

other conceivable subject. I left each time believing these men were wise beyond expectation, and I longed each time to return as soon as possible.

One not accustomed to the vigor with which these men pursued the conversation of the day might conclude that some ill will or hard feelings would result because of the tenor of the conversation and the level of noise. I knew better. These were friends who could personalize the discussion so that the friend to whom the particular comment was directed would get the point. They were quicker and more articulate than in any other place I heard them talk. I wondered why.

I concluded that it was the place. Something about that barbershop allowed these men to freely express themselves with all the depth necessary for the moment. There was nothing to inhibit them. I learned from these men. If I had not seen them and listened to them in this place, I would have assumed they were ordinary men doing ordinary things each day. I would have known nothing about their extraordinary capacity to deal with every situation if given the chance. They could have, if given the chance, competed in any arena. I did not know then that what was said there in that barbershop could not be repeated outside. In the 1950s, it was not allowed.

I think of that barbershop and the men who made it a special place for me as a child. For them it was a place where friends could gather and eloquently deal with a sometimes hostile world. For me, it was magic.

The shop is no longer there. A record shop sits in its place. The branch library, a few doors down, that those men inspired me to visit is not there, either. Sometimes when I pass Sixteenth and Martin Luther King Jr. Drive, I think maybe some of those wise men still gather and converse. Maybe.

Henry L. Jones Jr. is magistrate judge for the United States District Court, Eastern District. He is on the board of directors of the Arkansas Council of the National Conference of Christians and Jews. He and his wife, Pat Jones, currently live in Little Rock and have three children, Priscilla, Marcus, and Cameron.

SOUTHEAST ARKANSAS
A Father and Son Conversation

Jim Kelley

One of my favorite places in this state is a remote duck blind in southeast Arkansas. In December of each year, a good friend and I take our sons there for a weekend of hunting. The sun rising on a cold, clear morning, a mutual goal, and plenty of time dedicated to conversation with my son make that weekend and that place a special one.

As with so many "places," it is not the location but the people that make it a "favorite."

Jim Kelley is chairman
and president of First United
Bankshares in El Dorado.

MOUNT HOLLY CEMETERY

Lady Poets in Sundresses

Philip Martin

I have a friend who as a young woman just out of college spent a season living with relatives in New Orleans. Since her only credentials were an English degree, a fluttery sensibility, and a tender heart, employment was improbable, so after taking breakfast with the family each morning, she gathered up a stack of photocopied résumés and boarded the streetcar in a sundress. She went directly to St. Louis Cemetery No. 2, where she spent the afternoon amidst the crypts, scribbling poetry on the green-tinted pages of a stenographer's notebook.

Photo by Steve Keesee.

At least that is how I choose to remember the story. There is something about cemeteries that attracts lady poets in sundresses. I believe I have seen a few myself, pensively chewing their pens in the green peace of Little Rock's Mount Holly Cemetery.

It is situated on a hill near downtown, moated off by a humming strip of superhighway. Across the street is a car wash, and a few blocks away, the governor's mansion. At night, and sometimes during the day, you can on occasion hear the sad and tiny crack of gunfire from the rougher neighborhoods nearby.

But here there is reassurance. Here, people still have respect—mortality, finality commands it. Here rise the old granite and marble monuments; here lie little Cheopses and Ozymandiases, the decent and the dull, more than a hundred and fifty years' worth of the well brought-up and thought-of of our town. We put our dead in the ground here; we keep our ghosts tamped down by heavy hardware lest they get unruly.

It might seem morbid to love a graveyard, yet this place seems to me nothing less than a reliquary of human virtue and folly. There is humility and vanity and humor; beauty lurks in the broken faces of angels and in the moss that attaches to crosses.

It is quiet here, and calm. It is a splendid place for the lady poets to roost.

Born in Savannah, Georgia, Philip Martin is an Arkansan by choice. He writes for the *Arkansas Democrat-Gazette* in Little Rock. Martin was the executive editor of *Spectrum Weekly*, a Little Rock–based alternative newspaper, from 1989 to 1991. His work has also appeared in *Newsweek, Oxford American, New Times, Village Voice,* and dozens of other publications. A former baseball player and rock 'n' roll musician, he lives in west Little Rock with his wife, Karen, and two big stupid dogs.

ARKANSAS

A Place Called Talk

Jo McDougall

I couldn't know it until I left it, but I know it now. After eight years away from Arkansas, the thing I most miss in my sojourn here in the Midwest is not Arkansas as a place, as in trees, mountains, swamps, and bayous; it's not even that white humid summer light that hangs over the rice fields I grew up knowing in southern Arkansas or the lemony haze fingering the pines, oaks, and dogwoods along the pig trails of the Ozarks. What I miss most about Arkansas is the talk.

When Arkansans talk, they display an inborn need to dramatize, to keep an audience—even if it's only a flop-sprawled hound. They have a need to connect, and they will reel you, friend or stranger, into their worlds.

A few months ago, as I was unloading the trunk of my car at a Fayetteville, Arkansas, motel, a middle-aged couple who had parked beside me, also unloading their stuff, engaged me in conversation. In three minutes I heard the circumstances of the incredible amount of luggage in their trunk (the wife's fault); I heard about the man's sister-in-law's asthma; I learned where the couple had been that morning and the arguments they'd had and what they had eaten for breakfast. A third of it might have been true. It didn't matter. For a few moments strangers were kin, walking around in each other's stories. I knew then I was home; I knew then I'd been away too long.

But it's more than human connection that Arkansans seek when they talk. Most of the time, even in the most idle of conversations, they're aiming to enter into myth. One of my most memorable experiences of such alchemy occurred a year or so ago as I sat with dear friends, a man and his wife, as dusk made its dreamy way onto their sun porch. The man told a story of somebody who had just moved into this neighborhood of wide lawns and ferny porches that morning and had, that very evening, parked his pickup in the front yard, facing the street. What that action said to the rest of the enclave (Arkansans all) was that this newcomer had transgressed a ritual—some social, primal agreement—and was seemingly oblivious to it. They would have to set him straight. Myth from simple acts of life; on that porch, as the sun went down, I'd been in the presence of ancestral voices.

Talk, and the way they do it, is, I think, the difference between southerners, and especially Arkansans, and the rest of the world. Most people talk, much to their credit, to share ideas. Arkansans talk to make themselves and their listeners feel good; they talk to hear the old, shared stories.

This community of nonsense, alchemy, and myth can include the stranger, though, if one is willing to listen. The telling of a story even when there's not much of a story to tell is typical of the Arkansan, who, soon or late, will tell it to you, the visitor, in the parking lots, the small cafes, the filling stations across the state. If you listen you will hear almost any Arkansan above the age of three transform, with talk, the drab and ordinary of happenstance into mystery and shimmer, while wanting—indeed, almost commanding—you, stranger or friend, to enter there, also.

Jo McDougall is a poet who farmed with her husband near Stuttgart for several years and earned an M.F.A. degree from the University of Arkansas in Fayetteville. She teaches at Pittsburg State University in Kansas.

HOPE

A Pile of Sand

Rubye Blevins Rose (a k a Patsy Montana)

I am sure there will be much written about the beauties and the mysteries of the Ozarks and the Ouachitas. Their spectacular vistas always take my breath away. My favorite spot, though, is further south and intensely personal. I'm sure every reader will identify with what I am about to reveal, as we've all had, at some point in our life, a place that was ours all alone—a hidey hole, a place for Walter Mitty daydreams. In my case it was a pile of sand left by some long-departed ancient riverbed near our home place just outside of Hope.

I was born in a place long disappeared called Beaudry, down the road from Jesseville just north of Hot Springs. When I was about four we moved

to Hope. So this is really the only home I ever knew. This is where I graduated from high school in the old courthouse and won a brand-new automobile for selling the most newspaper subscriptions. And this is where my dreams started, not in the town itself, dear as it is in my memories, but in that pile of sand.

I grew up the only girl in a family of ten boys. My sandpile was my place of refuge, escape, and wild dreams of the future. I imagined all of the places that I would someday visit, strange and mysterious, and built castles as I imagined they would be. As I played, I dreamed of what I wanted to do with my life and sang the little songs that my mother had taught me. The time spent in that little sandpile set the whole course of my life. A few years later, when two of my brothers and I took one of Hope's famous watermelons to the World Fair in Chicago, my dreams from my sandpile began to come true. While there, I auditioned at WLS Radio, got the job, and the rest, as they say, is history.

My career has taken me all over the world, and I've been able to see real castles. But none has ever again inspired me as did those made of sand where I dreamed my first dreams outside my hometown of Hope. An appropriate name, don't you think?

Rubye Blevins Rose, a k a Patsy Montana, became the first country-and-western girl to have a million-selling record in 1935 with "I Want to Be a Cowboy's Sweetheart." According to Robert Cochran's *Our Own Sweet Sounds* (University of Arkansas Press, 1996), Patsy Montana "toured for fifteen years with the Prairie Ramblers, twenty-five years as a regular on the WLS Barn Dance" and "between 1934 and 1992, she made over seven thousand personal appearances in the U.S., Canada, and Europe." Patsy Montana died on May 3, 1996.

THE OLD STATE HOUSE
Dignity and Elegance

Ronnie A. Nichols

     One of my favorite places in Arkansas is our first state capitol building. Now called the Old State House, it is the oldest standing state capitol building west of the Mississippi River, and it beautifully personifies the dignity and depth of Arkansas's rich heritage. Constructed from 1833 to 1842, the timeless Greek Revival–style architecture retains its imposing elegance today, even though it is dwarfed by surrounding skyscrapers and hotels. Ironically, what we see and consider to be the front façade of this building was originally designed as the back entrance, with the grounds utilized as a public park. The front of the Old State House faces north to the Arkansas River, which emphasizes the state capitol's commanding place in the city.

The Old State House has played an important role in Arkansas's history, in part because all of Arkansas's working constitutions were written in its legislative chambers. It has been visited by noted figures such as Frederick Douglass and by presidents U. S. Grant, Theodore Roosevelt, and Benjamin Harrison. The Old State House gained worldwide recognition most recently as the stunning backdrop for President Bill Clinton's election-night victory speech in 1992. Today, the Old State House is a fully accredited museum of Arkansas's history and culture.

Ronnie A. Nichols is currently the director of the Old State House Museum and the Arkansas Commemorative Commission. He is a museum evaluator for the Institute of Museum Services in Washington, D.C. He has worked as a technical advisor with the Freddie Field's Production Company which filmed the motion picture *Glory* in Florida and Georgia. He resides in Little Rock with his wife, Sandra Bruce Nichols, M.D., and has one daughter, Marquise Nicole Nichols.

BOSTON MOUNTAINS

My Roots Are in Cass

Barbara Pryor

My favorite place in Arkansas? No way. There are so many of them, and they are all so diverse and special. I hardly know where to start.

David and I have traveled this magnificent state for over three decades. I recall some special thing about every county and courthouse, every pie supper, fish fry, bar-b-que, political rally, and graduation. I recall the Delta at sunset in the reddest light, the pine forests, the wolf and fox hunts.

I especially remember the days and nights going to and from, the short-cuts and byroads, the bridges, rivers, and streams that bind the state together—and always the people who weave a magic quilt of oneness that defines the character and soul of the state.

I'm a child of the hills. My roots are in Cass, in the Boston Mountains, where my great-grandmother (whom I call Grandmother) grew up on the Mulberry River. It's where her daughter and then her granddaughter—my mother, who never *knew* her mother—were also born. This has to be my favorite place of all.

My family were Turners, descended from Eli Turner of Turner Bend on Highway 23. He was reported to have fathered twenty-five offspring.

Bears used to roam within a few feet of the house and the pig trails. Legend has it that Jesse and Frank James rode those same trails, looking for who knows what kind of mischief. They are supposed to have spent the night at my grandmother's house.

For over 150 years, people have eked out a living among the rocks and hills that surround the Mulberry River. I left there—but not for good—at about the time my great-grandmother died. My memories of Cass will never leave me.

In spring the sky is as blue as a bird's wing. The new leaves meeting over the road are the palest green you ever saw—they're almost edible. Later, wild dogwood and redbud trees burst forth in the whitest and pinkest splendor.

In the summer the ground becomes a hardwood jungle. Fall is a time when the trees seem to be on fire with the strongest, earthiest colors. And in winter single trees stand bare against the light, as if made of the finest lace.

At night, all things grow country dark.

In my earliest memory I'm standing in my grandmother's yard, looking up at her flowers that were taller than I. And since she had a green thumb, everything she touched promptly grew—including children.

She cooked on a wood stove, and the main meal was at noon. There was a table full of vegetables, biscuits, chicken, ham, deer, and a peach cobbler made from peaches that came off one of her own trees. Supper was usually some kind of cornbread and cold milk, or ham wrapped in a biscuit. We ate on benches at a long table.

Grandmother grew her own tobacco and smoked it in a corncob pipe. I clearly remember the richness of the smells and the mix of wood smoke and tobacco.

The house was a log cabin with a screened-in porch running across the front. On one end was a grape arbor. This was my safe place.

There were three rooms in the house. The living room had iron beds and feather mattresses in each corner, a fireplace, rocking chairs, and coal-oil lamps. At night we were tucked in our beds, where we could listen to Grandmother and Mother talk and tell stories about the family. I recall their soft voices, and the laughter, and sometimes the tears.

They spoke of Grandmother's first husband, a young medical student who had smallpox and died. And they told stories of the Yankees who came and burned the barns and stole livestock.

Grandmother loved to tell the story of the day my mother came to live with her. She stood on the rock steps of her porch and watched a man carrying a child and leading another one by the hand. They walked through the middle of a huge field of corn that grew in front of her house.

The man was Grandmother's daughter's husband and not long a widower. He was bringing her two grandchildren for her to raise. He left them there on the porch, and when he had gone on his way, she gave the little girl her own name—Rosa Lee. That was my mother.

When I was a child, my mother would put my brother and me on a bus and tell the driver to take us to Turner Bend. The road was gravel then. We would spend the night at Uncle Champ's store and sleep on a pallet in the loft over the store.

The next morning he would drive us seven miles down the road where

Uncle Jake would be waiting with a flatbed wagon and a team of mules. We would ford the creek and go to Grandmother's house.

Grandmother collected bits of broken china and colored glass bottles and saved them for me. I would spend hours in the arbor's soft dirt, in the slanted light of the afternoon, endlessly arranging and rearranging the remnants.

We learned to swim in the cold green water of the Mulberry River. There was a large hollow rock where my mother would bathe my little brother. Sometimes we stayed in the creek all day long, and Mother would make coffee in a skillet, and we would drink it out of tin cups.

Years later, I took the same bus with my own young son and went to my great-grandmother's funeral in Ozark. She lived to be one hundred, and when she died she had some gray in her hair. But it was mostly still black as night—like my mother's when she died, and now like my son Mark's.

These days, when I turn off the interstate and onto Highway 23, no matter how tired I may be, I take a deep long breath of that sweet clean mountain air, and I drink the fresh cool water and feel restored. I know then that I'm home.

All of this brings me to Eudora Welty, one of my favorite writers, who remembered the hills of West Virginia in her book *One Writer's Beginning*. Here's how she recalled the feel of the landscape, so similar to my own:

"It took the mountain top, it seems to me now, to give me the sensation of independence. It was as if I'd discovered something I had never tasted before in my short life. Or rediscovered it—for I associated it with the taste of the water that came out of the well, accompanied with the ring of that long metal sleeve against the sides of the living mountain, as from deep down it was wound up to view brimming and streaming long drops behind it like bright stars on a ribbon. It thrilled me to drink from the common dipper. The coldness, the far, unseen, unheard springs of what was in my mouth now, the iron strength of its flavor that drew my cheeks in, fern-laced smell, all said mountain mountain mountain as I swallowed. Every swallow was making me a part of being here, sealing me in place, with my bare feet planted on the mountain and sprinkled with my rapturous spills. What I felt I'd come here to do was something on my own."

Barbara Pryor, a native of
Fayetteville and patron of
Arkansas artists, has spent
a great deal of time over the
past years in Washington,
D.C., where her husband
has been at work for the
state and the nation.

PORTLAND

A Sense of Place with a Strength of Differences

Robert D. Pugh

Boeuf Swamp, Dead Man's Bayou, and Bearhouse and Coon Creeks were, and are, on the perimeter of my favorite place in life as I have lived it for more than sixty years here in Portland, a tiny town located on U.S. Highway 165 and the Union Pacific Railroad in east Ashley County. Originally situated slightly to the west on meandering Bayou Bartholomew, its history began in the mid-1800s.

My first remembrances are of mud and dust, white and black people, horses and mules. Hard times and poverty were more the norm than comfortable surroundings. It was my whole life and only world as a young boy,

and I was infatuated and curious, loving every minute. It seems that I, along with everyone else, had a sense of place and belonging. I knew my world was bounded to the east by Boeuf Swamp and to the west by the hills and the "county seat." North and south limits were extended by the highway and trains, as far as Little Rock and Monroe, Louisiana. However, I thought that our town was the center and hub of the perimeter.

Boeuf Swamp, with its overflow of hardwoods to the east, gradually gave way to the higher sandy loam soil of Bayou Bartholomew as one came west to Portland. The rich loamy soil surrounding Portland, and stretching along both sides of Bayou Bartholomew, has been planted with cotton for more than a century. This fertile high ground has been our economic foundation and furnished the community with unusual opportunities over the last century. As a result, our town has for many years been a leader in cotton production and today is one of the more vibrant agricultural centers in Arkansas. Bayou Bartholomew has not only furnished us with rich farmland, but it has spawned several beautiful moss-laden cypress lakes nearby, such as Lake Grampus, Wilson Lake, and McCombs Brake. Only a few miles to the west is the coastal plain with vast pine forests and scattered small farms. Living with this geographic diversity in a rural setting enables one to become entwined in the beauty and spiritual renewal of the seasonal changes. This special world, as I first remember it, turns out to be somewhat of a microcosm of Arkansas geography.

When I was a child, Portland was the only place I had really known in the true sense of the word. Obviously, my world has grown considerably since those early memories, but my admiration of this community in rural Arkansas continues to grow as my experiences and horizons widen. It not only has diversity of geography but also of culture, being located in the bottom lands of Bayou Bartholomew, only a stone's throw from the forested coastal plain, with a significant black population and a small but growing Hispanic minority. Its social and political culture is heavily influenced by "the hills" due to their close proximity, larger area, and larger population. Because of these differences, we have developed as a community with civility, respect, and tolerance for one another and outsiders. It is a community that understates the extreme and exaggerates the mundane in colorful stories with dramatized examples. Having a close appreciation of this environment, through rural small-town living, makes one's life more interesting than ordinary and enables a person to keep a sense of perspective. Life here is lived with consideration, concern, and generosity, but still with recognition of the urgency for continued social changes and economic well-being. Maybe these are values of many small towns in rural America, but I feel that here they are cherished and nurtured with special care.

Robert D. Pugh is a fifth-generation native of Portland. He is engaged in farming and agribusiness in the Portland area and serves on the Entergy Corporation Board. He has served on the Portland School Board, the University of Arkansas Board of Trustees, and the Winthrop Rockefeller Foundation.

Photo by A. C. Haralson, Arkansas Department of Parks and Tourism.

Queen Wilhelmina

A Magnificent Mountain Retreat

Andree Layton Roaf

I have visited many beautiful and special places in our state since I became an Arkansan twenty-seven years ago. I have wonderful memories of family trips, especially the excitement of my children as we discovered new and different places to visit and things to do. But my family roots are deep in the mountains—the Blue Ridge Mountains of Northern Virginia. A part of my soul and heart will always remain there, and I never feel completely at home on flat land.

I can enjoy "doing nothing" as much as anyone I know. I never tire of gazing at the trees and listening to the singing of the birds in the woods which surround my home. At night, I like nothing better than to look up at the stars and to listen to the night in the woods around me—the whip-poorwill, the owl, the sounds of the large and small creatures moving about in the underbrush.

It is little wonder that I discovered the perfect place for me on a family trip some years ago to Queen Wilhelmina State Park near Mena. The beautiful Queen Wilhelmina Lodge allowed me to commune with nature, high atop Rich Mountain, while "doing nothing"—no telephone, no fax, no work, no roughing it (camping out entails far too much work to suit my tastes), no *television!* The view of the Ouachita Mountains is breathtaking. The nature trails allow you to leave behind even those few small intrusions of the world to be found in an isolated mountaintop lodge. The nights are quiet, serene, and a sense of being close to the heavens descends upon you even more than during the daylight hours.

There is a miniature railroad that circles the mountain, but that's okay; it fits. My children loved it, I loved it, and I look forward to taking my grandson there some day—to ride the train, to pet the animals at the animal park, but most of all, to experience the beauty of nature, high atop a mountain, far from the world, and close to the heavens.

Andree Layton Roaf is an associate justice on the Arkansas Supreme Court. She is the first African-American woman and only the second woman to serve on the court. Honored in the *Arkansas Business—Top 100 Women in Arkansas* in 1995, she lives in Pine Bluff with her husband, Dr. Clifton Roaf.

Photo by Tim Schick, Arkansas Department of Parks and Tourism.

PINNACLE MOUNTAIN
The Perfect Playground

Brooks Robinson

The first thought I have, when asked to name my favorite place in Arkansas, is of Pinnacle Mountain. Sitting an easy drive west of Little Rock, just south of the Arkansas River, it was the perfect playground for the Robinson family. When I was a youngster, my mom and dad would take my little brother Gary and me on a drive or sometimes a hike up the mountain; more often than not, three or four other kids in our neighborhood would be invited to go along with us—our dogs, too. At the top of the mountain we usually had a picnic.

My memories of those days, and of those scenes, are as clear to me as the photographs my mom still has of that special and peaceful place where we could see forever in all directions.

Even now, flying from time to time into Little Rock, I look down to see Pinnacle Mountain when we pass near it and that good feeling comes back again as I relive some moment out of the years of wonderful family times. To remember my childhood is to remember Pinnacle Mountain, to me the best of places in the best of states.

Brooks Robinson, affectionately referred to as "Mr. Baltimore Oriole," is a baseball Hall of Fame third baseman from Little Rock.

DESHA COUNTY

Preservation of the Past

Charlotte Tillar Schexnayder

Facing a rush of cool air which seems to come from nowhere on a sultry July afternoon, I shift on the makeshift bench of cypress in the dogtrot.

It is pleasant, though warm, and just the kind of setting for a reverie. "What," I ask myself, "is my favorite place in the Arkansas Delta?"

There are so very many, as mentally I roam over growing up and the ensuing years. Is it the Tillar Cypress Brake where those ancient cypress remind me they once protected the Quapaws?

Is it Huckleberry Hill, only a bluff for Bayou Bartholomew, but rich in memories of grapevine swings and childhood picnics?

Is it the Mississippi River levee from Pendleton to Arkansas City

where I can bounce along a gravel road and find serenity in the expanse of grazing lands, an occasional deer mingling with cattle, sometimes an eagle riding the currents overhead?

Is it the 1913 Tillar church where a whole community came together for a protracted revival embracing Methodists, Presbyterians, and Baptists in ecumenism, years before that word was popular?

Or is it the mile-after-mile expanse of white tufts a few days before the mechanical cotton pickers begin their harvest? Or geometrical patterns of rice levees in verdant shades?

As favorite as all these and other places are in the heart, there is still another. It is where I sit, for it is my roots in Desha County.

It hasn't been located here always, this two-story dogtrot house. Built before 1850 of hand-hewn eighteen-inch cypress logs, it was situated near Oakwood Bayou four miles east of Dumas.

I had heard its story for many years, but I first remember seeing this dogtrot house in 1954 when my mother, Bertha Terry Tillar, decided it had to be preserved. Then, a barn with little resemblance to a pioneer home, the dogtrot nevertheless brought forth a rush of family stories from my mother.

She had slept in a trundle bed in this log house before the turn of the century, but her favorite story concerned Mr. Frederick.

He was a German cabinetmaker who was tramping through the countryside when he arrived at the dogtrot where my great-grandfather Sam Terry and his family lived.

Mr. Frederick arrived on a Saturday. The Terrys asked him to rest and spend the night. On Sunday, he spent the day reading his Bible, for he didn't believe in traveling on the Lord's day. On Monday, the family liked him so much that he was asked to stay. And he did for forty years.

On the day my mother was born, May 15, 1892, Mr. Frederick hand carved a doll bed from walnut, cut from the immense trees which lined the lane to the house. That doll bed is carefully preserved in an exhibit in the Desha County Museum, where the dogtrot house is located. The house was moved, log by log, and reconstructed at the museum on Highway 165, Dumas, in the early 1980s when its former site was made into a soybean field.

This dogtrot, this place in my heart, is filled with more family stories than memories, for I never lived there. Each time I visit there, however, I know it ranks as a favorite of favorites.

A native of Tillar, Arkansas, Charlotte Tillar Schexnayder is president of Clarion Publishing in Dumas. She also is serving her sixth term in the Arkansas House of Representatives. In 1991–92, she became the first woman president of the National Newspaper Association in its 106-year history. She also has served as president of the National Federation of Press Women, Arkansas Press Women, Arkansas Press Association, Arkansas Professional Journalists, and the Dumas Chamber of Commerce. Schexnayder and her husband, Melvin, have published the *Dumas Clarion* for the past forty-two years.

Courtesy of Dixie Knight Photography.

Courtesy of Cranford, Johnson, Robinson, and Woods.

THAT BOOKSTORE IN BLYTHEVILLE
The World of Bookselling

Mary Gay Shipley

The place I most want to be in Arkansas is right where I am, at That Bookstore in Blytheville. What could be better—surrounded by the works of great writers, past and present. The store is a friendly, welcoming place for everyone. It provides the opportunity to meet an amazing variety of people—from the regulars who never let the week end without a visit to the one-time visitors who pass through Blytheville.

The stimulating challenge of the everyday operations of a nationally known bookstore, especially in a place where you would least expect it to be, is balanced by the interesting, creative people who work in the world of bookselling, writing, and publishing.

I never want to leave the company of this community: the volunteers who turn the back room into an elegant dining room complete with gourmet meals, the artists who perform here, the children who grow up here, the readers who discover new writers here.

That Bookstore in Blytheville has given me a way to return to Blytheville and to Arkansas a measure of what was given to me.

Courtesy of Cranford, Johnson, Robinson, and Woods.

Mary Gay Shipley was born and raised in Blytheville, Arkansas. She loves her hometown and has worked hard over the years to "Bloom Where Planted." She lives in the house built by her grand-father in 1907 and in which her father was born.

That Bookstore in Blytheville was created by Mary Gay Shipley to fill the vacuum that bookstore-less communities endure. She has been very active in the industry, having served on the board of directors and as an officer of the American Booksellers Association.

U.S. Highway 79

The Road Taken

Rodney Slater

My favorite place in Arkansas is really not a single spot, a plot of land, or a particular destination, but rather, of all things, a road—U.S. Highway 79. During my early years it was merely the roadway that passed before my home in Marianna, Arkansas, guiding others in their "pursuit of happiness." Over the years it has served for me as a stony road to cotton fields—in times when it seemed that hope, yet unborn, had died. Later, it was a country road to take me home to love and security and still later a yellow brick road taking me to lands of wonder and opportunity. Finally, it has served as a road to other roads, some diverged in a yellow wood, where the decision to take "the one less traveled" has "made *all* the difference."

Rodney Slater moved to
Arkansas from Mississippi and
served in several capacities,
including assistant attorney general and chairman of the State
Highway Commission, before
being named administrator
of the Federal Highway
Administration in 1993.

DOWNTOWN LITTLE ROCK

Acceptance, Tolerance, and Courage

Grif Stockley

My favorite place in Arkansas is the downtown area of Little Rock, but let me confess immediately I have a love-hate relationship with an arbitrary area that is bounded by Interstate 30 to the east, the state capitol on the west, Roosevelt Road to the south, and the Arkansas River to the north.

Guilty of what a friend of mine who lives downtown calls "institutional racism," I do not live in the area that I have described. When I think of living downtown (I have worked downtown for almost a quarter of a century

Photo by Tim Schick, Arkansas Department of Parks and Tourism.

and have never been robbed or mugged), at some point I get a mental picture of criminal activity, usually committed by black males. There is no doubt in my mind that this perception is unfair to every law-abiding African-American in Little Rock. It is a racial stereotype, a barrier to my own progress as a human being. My downtown friends argue that crime occurs in every neighborhood in Little Rock, and my own experience is that this perception is correct. When I lived west of University Avenue, my home was robbed. Still, my perception is that crime is much greater downtown, and I abhor the thought of living in fear, of having to be on guard, and of worrying about my property or personal safety. On the other hand, it may be simply that I am a physical coward and lack the courage of my convictions. Women, after all, routinely cope with the fear of being raped or assaulted. Why should I have a free ride?

Values developed while a Peace Corps volunteer in northern Colombia in the sixties have convinced me that life is more vivid, more meaningful, if it is an experience shared with others of different races, backgrounds, and economic levels. As my downtown friend Judith Faust has so eloquently expressed it,

Another aspect of my commitment to community is a belief in the richness of diversity. I don't want to live in a neighborhood that is all white and all middle-class. I'm white and middle-class. I know about white and middle-class. I want to live around people who are like me in those respects and who aren't. I like being around different folks who have more than I do and folks who have less, folks who are a different color than I, who maybe spoke another language before they spoke English, who are older than I, who make their living differently than I.

The thing is, I really do believe we're all in this together, and that to make it work, we have to know that and respect each other.

Downtown is where the passions of the city and state (during the '92 Clinton campaign, the nation) are vented: it is here we publicly declare ourselves as for or against, altruistically or selfishly. Downtown, for better or worse, is where the glue is mixed that attempts to bind us.

Blinded by the routine sameness of my route to work and a thousand personal concerns, I tend to ignore my surroundings. But if I concentrate on certain landmarks, the same messages reverberate inside my head. I turn off Markham onto Martin Luther King at the state capitol, and my psychic radar picks up the ghost of Orval Faubus. Perhaps it is my age (I was thirteen in 1957 when the state's most powerful and effective governor ever stamped onto the world's consciousness the image of Little Rock as a hateful, bigoted city.) that makes me obsess about Faubus's ghost, instead of, say, the larger-than-life appetites of Bill Clinton, who now dwarfs the memory of a master politician once thought to have no peer.

More than a stone's throw west on my daily commute (but not by much), at 600 West Capitol sit the federal judges (all Arkansans, we sometimes seem to forget) who for forty years have determined so much of our children's lives and consequently our own. The Little Rock School District's administrative offices are in the neighborhood at 810 West Markham, and the actions taken in these venues have incalcuable consequences for the rest of the city and the state, which has become a party to the endless litigation to enforce the Fourteenth Amendment's guarantee of equality for all Arkansan children.

History, I sense dimly in my rush to get to work, is all around me if I but realize it. A few blocks to the north on the banks of the Arkansas River at Markham and Center is the Old State House, scene on May 6, 1861, of a final convention vote on secession in which a single holdout, Isaac Murphy of Huntsville, kept the vote from being unanimous to dissolve our ties with the rest of the United States. Our history books record that in a tribute to his stubborn commitment to the country, Mrs. Frederick Trapnell, watching from the gallery, threw down to him a bouquet of flowers.

As I continue east on Capitol, I begin to realize that downtown is practically the only place left in Little Rock where we as citizens can determine if the American experience can still be about diversity and not sameness. Granted, many have no interest in this experiment. There are those of us who are completely happy in the burbs, and the closest we want to come to people not like ourselves is the television news to confirm that America is cracking and splitting before our eyes into two contiguous but borderless countries—one an underclass, often African-American, composed of the working poor and the unemployed and spiraling downward to an abyss composed of the homeless, persons with mental illness, alcoholics, derelicts, gangs, and drug pushers and their customers, some of whom are prone to violence and all to hopelessness. The other country is predominantly white, relatively affluent, and concerned with law and order and property values. As I walk from the parking lot at Sixth and Louisiana to the Hall Building on Capitol, I realize that downtown Little Rock is where these two countries intersect.

From Marianna in the Delta, I told myself that I was moving in 1972 not only to the state capital, but to an urban area. Little Rock would provide experiences that small-town Arkansas lacked, including a downtown that was alive with shops, theaters, restaurants: in short, the diversity that only a dense, eclectic urban environment can provide. Moving here permanently after Law School in Fayetteville to look for a job and to take the bar examination, I was excited about what I thought I would find. Marianna was a great place to grow up for an unconscious, white, middle-class kid in the 1950s. It was as safe and friendly an environment as a rigidly segregated system, and all that it entailed, can provide. I called the black man who cut our grass "Andrew," and he called me "Mr. Griffin." I don't recall my parents routinely locking our house or vehicles. As a junior and senior in high school I covered sports for the town weekly paper, the *Courier Index,* but it never occurred to me to ask the editor and publisher if I could cover a single game of the Moton Lions (though we shared the same football field) and who hopefully had better athletes. In those days, the failure to acknowledge that another race with its own schools made up a good portion of the Delta was so ingrained that I would refer to the Marianna Porcupines, the Forrest City Mustangs, or the Helena Indians, instead of writing, for example, "the T. A. Futrall Porcupines lost last night."

My two-year stint in the Peace Corps and a subsequent visit to New York City broadened my horizons a bit. I wasn't quite ready for the Big Apple, but Little Rock seemed the place to be to work and enjoy the city.

In 1972 I began a job as a staff attorney in Little Rock with the Legal Aid Bureau of Pulaski County. Our office was located at the corner of Sixteenth and Broadway. At noon and during breaks I walked around the neighborhood on Gaines and Arch Streets and discovered for the first time the astonishing ninteenth-century homes in this area. Though no guidebook then existed to tell me what I was looking at (the first was published in 1976 by the Quapaw Quarter Association), I was flabbergasted by the size of such homes as the Hemingway House at 1720 Arch and the Plunkett House across the street. Yet these homes were then serving as multifamily units for people, many black, some or most of whom surely qualified to be clients at Legal Aid.

In 1977, the Legal Aid Bureau of Pulaski County moved into the Hall Building at 209 West Capitol and became Central Arkansas Legal Services. Centrally located for our clients because of the bus lines, we have remained here ever since, changing our name in 1996 to the Center for Arkansas Legal Services as we merged with another legal service program. I was personally delighted with the move because it was in the smack-dab middle of the city, and although I realized that the downtown retail and entertainment area was mostly gone, I was encouraged by the efforts to revitalize it. Twenty years later, I still am.

But what had happened to downtown? When I was twelve, I remember driving over to Little Rock with my future brother-in-law and thinking I had been in a real city. Granted, it didn't rival the downtown of Memphis where the more affluent whites in eastern Arkansas often went to shop, but still it was impressive to a kid from Lee County.

Not a historian, I do not pretend to understand fully the precise causes of the decline of downtown Little Rock. It is not that there is a dearth of opinion on the subject of urban blight. Other cities' downtowns have decayed and died. But as with so many subjects involving human motivation, the explanations one hears and reads tend to reflect the values and concerns of whoever is doing the explaining.

For people of my generation the heyday of downtown Little Rock was clearly in the 1950s. Interestingly, Jewish merchants dominated the scene along Main Street. The department stores bearing the names of Cohn, Pfeifer, and Blass put smaller stores like J. C. Penney's and Sears & Roebuck in the shade. A fascinating book published in 1994 on the history of the Jewish experience in Arkansas reports that approximately one-fourth of the 160 merchants and store owners who belonged to Downtown Little Rock Unlimited in July of 1960, a group organized to hold the line against the migration out west, was Jewish. Headed by Sam Strauss Jr., whose family was the owner of Pfeifer's of Arkansas department stores, Downtown Little Rock Unlimited had good reason to be worried. The malls were coming! In April of 1956, Town and Country Shopping Center, at the corner of Hays (now University) and Asher, was described as "Little Rock's first integrated shopping center with all the stores under one roof." Meant to accommodate the Broadmoor residential development of seven hundred homes started by Fausett and Company in 1953, Town and Country was, of course, a little squirt in what were to be some big buckets.

In the fifties the country was into "urban renewal," which sometimes seemed merely to mean the destruction of old buildings and the erection of parking lots. The local authors of *How We Lived: Little Rock As an American City,* report that the Central Little Rock Urban Renewal Project "envisioned a complete reshaping of downtown Little Rock with expressways and vast parking areas to accommodate motorists coming into the area and modern high-rise apartment and office buildings for those living and working downtown." The authors note that many of the goals were accomplished, a fact today confirmed in an eyeblink.

Poverty (and not the kind liberals and conservatives can argue about) haunts downtown Little Rock like a specter. Capitalism and democracy collide in front of my office every day. My own failures as a lawyer for poor people confront me. At noon, as I walk about the area, the homeless, persons with mental illness, alcoholics, and drug addicts dare me to look at them. Often I try not to, because I know I will often be panhandled unless I hurry by and make no eye contact. As one of the attorneys who once successfully challenged the constitutionality of the state's involuntary civil commitment and criminal commitment statutes, and thus made it more difficult to commit and confine the mentally ill, all too frequently I see my former clients, emaciated and ill, on the street. The absolute bottom (I hope) came one day when a former client, whom I got out of Rogers Hall (then the state maximum security unit for the criminally insane), was shot and killed by police on Capitol Avenue. He had boarded a bus downtown and was armed with a machete (though no one was harmed). My first reaction was to blame the Little Rock police for not handling the situation better. My second was to wonder about my own culpability in getting people out of the state hospital when there were few services for them in the community.

In the fall of 1995 I personally witnessed two incidents (and had a third reported to me by a coworker) of harassment of young black males by a policeman. It is not a crime for a young, male African-American to wait for a bus downtown, even if it is in front of a store that has complained to the police about panhandlers and drunks scaring customers away. For the first time, I had an inkling of how outraged I would be if I had been in the shoes of the individuals who respectively were ordered to move down to the bus stop on Center, arrested, and, in the case of the third, frisked.

Most of us want the poor and other misfits to be neither seen nor heard and, when they must, to be polite and grateful to the rest of us for suffering their existence. When I'm off the clock, I know I do. One of my favorite places to read in Little Rock at noon was the minipark next to the public library on Louisiana between Seventh and Eighth. Its fountain and sculpture made it a delightful place to sit in the sun and eat lunch. Despite usually being panhandled, most times it was worth it if only because of the exquisite view of St. Andrews Cathedral on the corner. Today, this concrete oasis has an iron fence protecting it from the public. There were too many humans in rags sleeping, drinking, urinating, and doing all the other socially undesirable things that those at the bottom of society's barrel do. Damn it, they took away my park. But who was "they"? Was it the poor who didn't act nice enough, or was it the beleaguered library staff who already serve as hosts for the homeless?

Do I have a moral obligation to share the city with others, or is it permissible to feel, as a tax-paying citizen, I should not have to be subjected to the discomfort and danger of living and working in a free society? As I stand gazing sadly at the iron bars, I do not have to look far to see the sources of my irritation. The First Presbyterian Church at Eighth and Scott operates the Stewpot and feeds hungry people at noon, and Our House, also supported privately, at Eighth and Louisiana provides a few homeless people a place to stay. Government has always been a convenient target for my anger, but today as I look toward the library at the homeless men resting against the wall, I can't figure out how to blame it without admitting that any solution I would devise carries its own problems.

Often, my inclination is to censor human nature and blame government for it, and I get support from neighborhood activists and civil-rights advocates who make a forceful case that historically developers and their allies at city hall have all too often ignored downtown at the expense of the poor and the African-American population. It is beyond dispute that the city has annexed huge areas to the west and that many resources have been allocated to their expansion. Motivations such as "racism" and "greed" are offered, in part, to account for these developments. I am reminded that Little Rock is approximately 30 percent African-American. Few disagree that

Little Rock was an officially and unofficially racially segregated city until the 1950s and some time after that in varying degrees. Arguably, in some areas, it still is. Certainly, we are emotionally segregated from each other.

Others see few, if any problems, in the stampede to the west. Market forces should determine where the resources of the city are spent. If the downtown area completely deteriorates and dies, then some may remember to send flowers, but many businessmen and developers these days will be too busy developing Chenal Parkway and beyond to attend the funeral.

Yet, in 1996 there is an air of hope downtown. I look forward to walking to the exciting new River Market which is under construction. Across the river there will be a new arena. The Little Rock convention center is being expanded. The Museum of Natural Science and History will be a knockout. I can't wait for the new library to be finished.

In recent years the city has modified its form of government to require mostly ward representation, giving power to people who are directly accountable to their own neighborhoods. The city has worked hard to create and strengthen neighborhood associations. Housing code enforcement has been made a priority, and there are two neighborhood alert stations downtown to deal more effectively with crime.

My downtown friends somehow refuse to give up their idea that Little Rock is a community best appreciated through experiencing and accepting differences, not similarities. I admire them for their commitment. If they sometimes seem in denial or defensive, then welcome to the club. The philosophy that "we are all in this together" is such a minority position these days that it is refreshing to hear my friends praise virtues that today almost seem quaint in a society where people anonymously tap buttons on their keyboards and think they are truly communicating with each other. I don't think I am putting words in the mouths of my downtown friends by suggesting that communication at its most meaningful level among humans involves personal risk and is not merely an intellectual enterprise. It involves acceptance, tolerance, and courage. One of these days I may be up to it.

Grif Stockley is the author of four novels: *Expert Testimony, Probable Cause, Religious Conviction,* and *Illegal Motion.* Though marketed by his publisher (Simon & Schuster) as mysteries, Stockley prefers to characterize his books as "lawyer novels." All are set in Arkansas and follow the travails of Gideon Page, a widower who is in solo legal practice in "Blackwell County," which his local readers immediately recognize as Little Rock. To convey what Stockley is attempting with this series, a quote from a *Publishers Weekly* review (December 20, 1993) of *Religious Conviction* states: "The action occurs in Arkansas, but this novel's spiritual territory is Graham Greene country: the plot involves religion, suicide, and pornography. Although the author's jauntily colloquial prose is nothing like Greene's, the two writers also share a preoccupation with their characters' moral dilemmas. Stockley (*Expert Testimony*) is more interested in ideas than thrills . . ." Grif Stockley's fifth novel, *Blind Justice*, will be published by Simon & Schuster in August of 1997.

CAMDEN

Home Is Not the Same

Carl Stover

Before Daddy died there were cattle on the place, and we always harvested a crop of hay. There were turkeys (never as good as Butterballs), guineas, and chickens. The sounds of the day rang truer than our clocks and governed our hours with a synchronization that seemed natural. I admit I have never gotten used to any other controls for my waking and sleeping.

Now that he is gone, we hardly know what to do with the land. There isn't much—only forty acres plus the homeplace. Right now a cousin uses it for his cattle and hay in exchange for a beef a year. We've thought about putting it all in pines for the paper mill. I say I am going to look into it, but

Mama and my brother still live in the house, and they like to see the pastures more like they used to be, so I haven't checked with the paper company.

The farm is not far from the Ouachita River, just outside of Camden, about a hundred miles south of Little Rock. The land has just enough roll to be interesting. Daddy built all the barns and fences with help from me and my brother. The barns and sheds have sheltered hay, tools, field vermin, lovers, the broken hearted, playing grandchildren, and now, family reunions. The land around the farm belongs to one cousin or another—land given or left to them by my uncles or aunt who got the land from my grandparents when they divided the big farm and homeplace my mother's father had acquired. Tradition was that all the children, but the baby, got acreage; the baby got the homeplace. And that's what happened. Tradition also has it that the farms never go to in-laws; they pass down directly to the offspring, and everyone's will reads that way.

Every visit home satisfies my need to be connected with my extended family: to hear about their exploits and be served the fruits of the land—fish, duck, venison, barbecue, and home-ground corn meal—which feeds more than just my body. Even the in-laws (including my wife) not raised in this region of the state like to experience the crafts of the area and spend their time searching for river-bottom antiques, beautiful quilts, and any local history that can shed light on the children begat of marriages to those who grew to adulthood in this unique place.

I still don't know what I will do with the farm when the time comes. Right now I don't have to make a decision. When my grandsons visit, they sleep on the old bunk beds that look out over the main pasture where they run, play in the tall grass, and try to be brave enough to get close to the cows. They see the look of the early morning dew and hear my cousin's cows, and they build memories similar to mine.

Mama said she will not buy any more guineas or turkeys after these are gone. Wild animals steal them away one by one. Nothing is done with them—they just make the expected noises at the right times. My uncle comes and feeds them because my mother and brother can't get around very well, so really, the guineas are an imposition hard to say goodbye to.

We never worked at the paper mill. When I became an engineer, my family hoped I would come back to Camden to work and build on a good site on the farm. My grandmother said I could "get on regular" at the paper mill. But I had never seen the world, and so I went to California instead. Now that I have seen much of the world, I come back to my favorite place—

the farm, close to the Ouachita River and the small town of Camden, where I grew up with the smells of the paper mill, helping my dad. Now he is gone, though, it isn't quite the same.

Camden was originally known as *Écore à Fabri* (Fabry's Bluff), the name taken from a Frenchman who was engaged in trafficking up and down the Ouachita River, trading powder and lead to the settlers and Indians for furs. In 1843 the name was changed to Camden at the suggestion of a settler who had moved from Camden, Alabama.

The key to early development of this area was its access to New Orleans' markets by way of the water routes of the Ouachita and Mississippi Rivers. Timber and cotton demands stimulated and supported numerous sawmill enterprises and cotton farms. A local entrepreneur operated a successful stagecoach line, connecting Memphis, Tennessee, through Camden, to the southwest frontier.

Camden was a Confederate outpost during the Civil War and suffered considerable deprivation as local resources were exhausted in the delivery of supplies to the rebel army. The area was the scene of several skirmishes, notably the Battle of Poison Spring, and monuments and historic buildings are maintained to commemorate this era.

After the Civil War, the network of south Arkansas villages was somewhat rearranged by the coming of the Cotton Belt Railroad, but timber and cotton continued as principal economic drivers. Oil discovery created a short-lived flurry of excitement, with several young wildcatters getting their start before moving on to the major fields and fortunes to be found in Oklahoma and Texas. During World War II, the woodlands on the other side of the river were developed as a manufacturing site, a naval ammunition depot, and a training base for army pilots.

The Ouachita River basin of south Arkansas continues as a mixture of rich farmland and large tracts of loblolly and yellow pine, with the timberland generally owned or leased by paper companies. Small farms and small towns dominate the area. Not far to the west is the Washington Post restoration of the first Arkansas capital, and Hope, Arkansas, the birthplace of President Bill Clinton.

As a member of Marshall Space Flight Center, in Huntsville, Alabama, Carl Stover manages NASA's global communications networks, providing data, voice, and video services to NASA centers, contractors, and international partners in performance of space flight, aeronautics, and science research programs. He graduated from the University of Arkansas in 1959 with a degree in mechanical engineering.

THE WHITE RIVER
The River That Can't Be Tamed

Billy Joe Tatum

I never chose to live in the Ozarks. I chose to live with my husband, who chose to live here. I have learned to love this Ozark Plateau, its calming spirit, its wildness, its abundant flora and fauna. On a cool quiet morning at Sylamore, the fog rises through tall, rough sunflowers as our canoe glides silently on the White River. Though the river has changed immeasurably since Henry Schoolcraft journeyed here in 1819, it's still exciting.

Gliding near the river's edge we see a mink family skitter through a stand of cardinal flowers and slink under the roots of a willow tree. As we pass stark, rugged bluffs, an eagle soars upward from an outcropping covered with gnarled, aged cedars. Deer are spotted feeding in grassy meadows studded with blue asters and goldenrod. Wild turkey can be heard and occasionally seen.

A heronry, miles down the river, is now abandoned, but some sixty rough, twigged nests still crown the large sycamore trees. Many of the great blue herons fishing along the banks among log jams hatched here. Arkansas's White River is not the wilderness river of Schoolcraft's day, but it's still wild enough for exploration.

Billy Joe Tatum, an herbalist and author in Mountain View, is known for her cookbooks using plants available in the wild.

BEAR CREEK LAKE

Nature at Close Range

Harold Wiegand

My favorite outdoor destination in eastern Arkansas is Bear Creek Lake, located on Highway 44, eight miles south of Marianna in Lee County. This 625-acre jewel is wholly within the boundaries of the 20,946-acre St. Francis National Forest and offers excellent fishing, camping, hiking, picnicking, and the opportunity to observe nature at close range.

Bear Creek Lake is a highland reservoir with fairly deep water and numerous quiet, secluded coves and fingers. Situated near the southern tip of Crowley's Ridge, it bears little resemblance to the cypress-draped shallow-water oxbow lakes typically found in Arkansas's Delta region. Its nearly

sixty miles of hardwood-timbered shoreline teems with all manner of animals and birds. Although there are some weekend and vacation cottages on the two larger lake arms, most of the area is pristine and offers a peaceful retreat from the day-to-day urban rat race.

Quietly boating into one of the many shady coves, one may see deer, turkey, raccoon, otter, beaver, heron, and a myriad of other species of wildlife. There are always various types of snakes present on dead trees, logs, and stumps, the most prevalent being the water moccasin; however, if unmolested, these reptiles usually give people a wide berth.

The lake offers excellent fishing for bass, bream, crappie, and catfish, without the clamor of high-powered boats and jet skis. It is a perfect place to launch a small boat or canoe for a day of angling or leisurely exploration.

Although Bear Creek Lake is not far from Helena and Memphis, it remains relatively unspoiled. It has been my favorite getaway spot for more than fifteen years, and I go there whenever I can to recharge my mental batteries.

Harold Wiegand, fifty-five, is a
retired U.S. Air Force officer living
in Cabot, Arkansas. His favorite
activities include hunting, fishing,
and camping.

FLAT ROCK

Awash in Beauty and Innocence

Lucinda Williams

Twenty years ago the world seemed as young as we were. There were four of us, delighting in freedom and friendship. The place—a special, mostly secret, and wholly unforgettable place—we know only as Flat Rock. It lay southeast of Fayetteville, near Elkins and Durham, just off Highway 16. We scrounged gas money to get there.

You couldn't go all the way by car; it was a pretty good walk from the nearest road, through a couple of gates, across a big hayfield, then into a small woods that opened up to a creek.

A sign by the gate said, "It's OK to come in but please protect the environment." We never did learn whose land it was by law; it became ours in spirit, and we cared for it lovingly.

The stream made its way across the hilly countryside, spilling over at one shady spot into a quiet pool, wide and deep enough for wading, then running on toward a convergence with other creeks to form the White River.

A stair of fieldstones led down to the pool. On the hottest days of summer we'd have to splash water on the rocks so they wouldn't burn our bare feet. The pond was clear and cool. Some of us would walk upstream, past a little rapids, and tube down. No one wore anything into the water. Our clothes waited along the bank, some neatly folded, some in piles. We laughed a lot. It was the purest joy I've ever known, there with my friends in a spot of such beauty, peacefulness, and innocence that we felt beautiful, too, and innocent and peaceful. And we were, for a while.

Lucinda Williams lived in Fayetteville before her career in country rock took her to Nashville. Among the several honors for her work are a BMI award, a Nashville Music Award, and a Grammy.

COTTER

At a Minor Bend on the White

C. D. Wright

I was sent a panoramic view of Cotter in the mail. Now that I am recalling the photo, it cannot be found, but I know that it was taken prior to the 1930s because the bridge built by the WPA across the White River is not in place. In the accompanying letter, Mother wrote, "I bet you didn't know Cotter was a peninsula."

The cold cold cold White will forever be my mind's eye of a river— a real river.

The WPA bridge, with three lamplit arches, is a bridge by which the Golden Gate, the London, the Brooklyn, the Pont Neuf, the Bridge of San

Photo by A. C. Haralson, Arkansas Department of Parks and Tourism.

Luis Rey, and other famous spans dim by comparison. I just call it the Cotter Bridge, my parents' Ponte Vecchio, where my mother succeeded in nabbing my father's attention by dropping little stones onto the heads of the couple sparking below.

Parallel to the two-lane car bridge is the railroad bridge, the same my great-grandfather died constructing and my cousin fell from when sniffing the foggy night from the jostling caboose. A KOA camper brought his banged-up body to shore. My star-kissed cousin Terry talked and walked to tell of it.

The spring. Just below the bridge by the trout dock is where the locals swam. Cold cold. And clear, sharp-rock-bottomed. My lips went instantly blue and my feet winced, but I was unutterably glad to be there. Lightning struck the overhanging tree, and that was the end of the tree swing until the townsfolk erected a steel girder to replace the oak. Of course, the new swing was not the same. It cast only a mean girder of shade.

The Colonial Hotel. Probably already a residence hotel in my childhood. I often went there with Mamo and Papo for family-styled Sunday dinners.

Roy's grocery. Where my Uncle Sneed surprised my Mamo by coming in from California on leave. The way he told it, "She liked to tore the meat counter down when I came up behind her, and said 'Hey, Mom.'"

Richmond's Store: *If we don't have it, you don't need it.* Dad always bought a stick of horehound candy, a taste I did not acquire. I bought sassafras. But if it was a leg you lacked, you could buy a prosthesis, or a bolt of dotted swiss for some look-alike dresses, or a set of ruby tea glasses. Only Carr's in Berryville could rival its all-but-exhaustive inventory.

The dirt-floored jailhouse by the tracks. The source of a thousand-and-one lurid tales.

The depot. The site where all once-lively towns turn into museums.

There is no more business downtown; there is no movie house, no lumber yard, no hardware, no hotel, no passenger car. Some of the old native rock buildings have been serviced back into use by a German manufacturer of work uniforms. How he discovered Cotter, I will never know, but prosper there he does.

At Christmas, Cotter's two main streets were strung in parallel streams of blue lights. Only blue. A sort of evening-in-Paris theme.

Mamo's root cellar was a scary place, but my cousin Pamela Jo and

I loved to play on top of it, and around Papo's johnboat. Their day-lilies, their rock garden, their screen porch. A black iron washpot eventually traveled from Mamo's backyard across the street to Aunt Mildred's where it continues to gush leggy geraniums.

Vacation Bible School. Wednesday night Sunbeamers. If you stayed at Mamo's on a Wednesday or a Sunday you went to church. Brother Finn was loud and weepy and sweaty. His parish both loved and pitied him. He embarrassed me, but I lay my head in Mamo's lap with my half-stick of Juicy Fruit and calmed to the stroke of her hand in my hair. Back home we were slack. Episcopalian.

My cousin and I played paper dolls for hours at a stretch. Aunt Mildred was so fastidious I thought she tortured her children with hygiene. The house smelled of disinfectant. In Cotter even grown-ups had bed dolls which wore elaborate crocheted ball gowns. Lavender was the preferred color of yarn.

The path on the bluff was a necessary trek. Careful, copperhead territory. And hardwoods: oak, hickory, walnut, redbud, dogwood, maple, serviceberry. Maidenhair dripped down the mineral-stained rock.

My uncle, the second of four generations of railroad workers on my mother's side, was a Missouri-Pacific brakeman. Heading home on the Redball, he never tired of rounding the final bend toward Cotter, especially after frost.

The trout docks. My most sustaining idyll of employment for poets is being a guide on a White River trout dock. Running the bait shop on weekdays, selling night crawlers and pork skins. Okay, renting videos and Nintendo games.

An adobe motel on the bluff. The name of it is lost to me now. It had already gone belly up when I was little, but it remains my idea of a seaside villa. I thought I would someday own the failing venture. Not in order to make it thrive, but to fill it with books and paintings and long-haired cats and loud, asocial music, and to tolerate the occasional stranded traveler. There I would write my monster poem.

Mother took a float trip just last year with another Baxter County woman. I'm in heaven, her friend kept saying as they drifted along the great bluffs; this is heaven, as the guide cooked their rainbow trout over an open fire, as the little rock towns on the banks slid in and out of sight. Heaven.

Photo by Forrest Gander.

C. D. Wright is a poet and
publisher. She grew up in
Harrison, took her M.F.A.
degree from the University of
Arkansas in Fayetteville, and
teaches at Brown University in
Rhode Island. She is coauthor of
*The Lost Roads Project: A Walk-
in Book of Arkansas,* a literary
guide to the state history.

My Favorite Place

_____
_____
_____
_____
_____
_____
_____
_____
_____
_____
_____

161